ISBN 978-1-332-19827-6
PIBN 10297019

English
Français
Deutsche
Italiano
Español
Português

www.forgottenbooks.com

Mythology Photography **Fiction**
Fishing Christianity **Art** Cooking
Essays Buddhism Freemasonry
Medicine **Biology** Music **Ancient
Egypt** Evolution Carpentry Physics
Dance Geology **Mathematics** Fitness
Shakespeare **Folklore** Yoga Marketing
Confidence Immortality Biographies
Poetry **Psychology** Witchcraft
Electronics Chemistry History **Law**
Accounting **Philosophy** Anthropology
Alchemy Drama Quantum Mechanics
Atheism Sexual Health **Ancient History**
Entrepreneurship Languages Sport
Paleontology Needlework Islam
Metaphysics Investment Archaeology
Parenting Statistics Criminology
Motivational

Songs
of the
Workaday World

by
Berton Braley

New York
George H. Doran Company

TO

M. R.

THIS LITTLE COLLECTION IS DEDICATED.

MY thanks and acknowledgments are due to the following magazines and publishers for permission to use these poems in book form:

The Saturday Evening Post, Technical World Magazine, Power, Harper's Weekly, The Edison Monthly, The American Machinist, Coming Nation, Popular Magazine, The Cavalier, Collier's Weekly, Adventure, Puck, McClure's Magazine, Newspaper Enterprise Association, La Follette's Weekly, Woman's World, Ainslee's Magazine, The Designer, and the New York Telephone Company.

CONTENTS

CONTENTS

SONGS OF THE TRUE ROMANCE

SONGS OF THE WORKADAY WORLD

THE MIRACLE WORKER

THE "Dreamers of Empire" travel in style
  On a glitterin' palace car,
An' they look with a dignified, scornful smile
  On the kind of men we are;
They pay us the smallest pay they dare
  An' call us a "frowsy crew."
But they know—an' a hell of a lot they care—
  We're making their dream come true.

    Work and women an' fight,
      Dice an' women an' drink;
    A spree on pay day night
      A day or two in the clink—
    A fine old life to live,
      An' a low down life, says you?
    But we ain't dreamin' no dreams ourselves,
      We're makin' your dreams come true.

Presidents ponder an' managers scheme,
  But we are the guys who sweat
Creatin' the real thing outen' the dream
  An' doin' it right, you bet!
We loaf when we kin and work when we must,
  Our morals is mighty few,
But winter an' summer, snow er dust,
  We're makin' the dream come true.

THE MIRACLE WORKER (continued)

> Hogan an' Schmitz an' Jones,
>   Levisich, Schwank, LeBeau,
> Talkin' in heavy tones
>   Wotever Lingo they know;
> Dago an' French, an' Russ,
>   Irish an' English, too—
> Hairy an' hard an' coarse an' rough,
>   Makin' the dream come true!

There ain't no medals run off for us,
    We're tickled to get our pay,
An' there ain't no papers making a fuss
    When some of us pass away;
We're nothin' but hoboes from hobo town
    Puttin' the railroad through,
Cuttin' the cliffs an' the mountains down,
    An' makin' the dream come true.

> The big bugs git the cash
>   An' most of the praise an' fame:
> We git our pay an' our daily hash
>   An' nobody knows our name.
> But it's all in the chance we take
>   The job that we've got to do,
> We haven't no time fer dreams ourselves,
>   We're makin' your dream come true.

THE STEEL-WORKER

WHEREVER new bridges are flinging
    Their spider-web skein to the skies;
Where the steel ships are made for the business of
    trade;
    Where the skyscrapers gauntly arise;
Where the cranes lift the twenty-ton girders
    And the red rivets hiss through the air—
From Chile to Nome and from China to Rome,
    The steel-worker's sure to be there.

      "Hey you!"
        (So the foreman said)
      "Watch the way you're doin' there;
        Use your bloomin' head.
      Lower her! Now—let 'er go!
        Ram the rivets through."
      (That's the way they do the job,
        Do it proper, too.)

This week you will find him on Broadway
    Some forty floors upward or so,
Where the men seem to crawl on just nothing at all
    When you watch from the sidewalk below.
Next week he'll be starting for Egypt,
    This viewer of cities and men,
With his money all spent he is fully content
    So long as he's moving again.

THE STEEL-WORKER (continued)

"Hey you!"
(Hear the foreman call)
"Swing her over—hold her there!
Hoist a bit—that's all.
Drop her now, but drop her slow.
Now you've got her true."
(That's the way they do the job,
Do it proper, too.)

His passport's the card of his union
Wherever he happens to land,
His home is the spot where a job's to be got,
For the skill of his head and his hand;
No task is too distant to tackle,
No chance too outlandish or dim;
He carelessly goes like the wind as she blows,
And the world has no terrors for him.

"Hey you!"
(Hear the foreman shout)
"Watch that girder overhead!
Clear the Way—LOOK OUT!
Hi, you fool, get out o' that!
Almost got him—whew!"
(That's the way they do the job,
Do it proper, too.)

THE JUNGLE JOB

I SAID to myself, "I am through pioneering,
  I'm sick of the wilderness, lonely and rough,
I'm sick of the grader's camp built in a clearing,
  I'm weary of laborers hairy and tough;
I'm tired of the outfit—the bed and the ration—
  The steam-shovel's puffing, the shock of the blast.
I want to go back where there's civilization,
  The fun and the frolic I knew in the past.

  "The life that has savor and vim in
    The sights and the noises of towns,
  The laughter and lure of the women,
    The glitter of jewels and gowns;
  I'm done with this business forever,
    I'm off to see 'cities and men.'
  And, once I have landed, I'll never
    Come back to the jungle again!"

So I made for the city of wonder and glamor—
  The city whose glory had shone in my dreams.
I plunged with delight in its hurry and clamor,
  Its welter of hopes and ambitions and schemes.
I reveled again in its food and its raiment,
  The music and lights and the gay-hearted mirth,
And I said to myself, "There is no form of payment
  Can tempt me again to the outposts of earth!"

THE JUNGLE JOB (continued)

But in spite of the pleasuring places,
· In spite of the vast city's thrill,
The spell of the unconquered places
Came following after me still;
At night it would suddenly wake me,
By day it would whisper—and then
I knew it was trying to make me
Come back to the jungle again.

I had thought that the splendors of cities would tame
me;
I fought with the thrall of a life I reviled;
But the lure of the game I had played overcame me—
The battle with nature far out in the wild!
The fleshpots were sweet—but they never could hold
me.
I packed up my kit and I made for the trail,
And now I believe what the old-timers told me,
The spell of the wilderness never can fail!

I'm back to the "furthermost farness,"
I'm way, way "ahead of the steel";
I'm wearing my engineer's harness,
The gravel is under my heel;
The dreams of the city still bind me,
The call of it comes to my ken,
Yet somehow I left it behind me,
I'm back to the jungle again!

THE POWER PLANT

WHIRR! Whirr! Whirr! Whirr!
  The mighty dynamos hum and purr,
And the blue flames crackle and glow and burn
Where the brushes touch and the magnets turn.
Whirr! Whirr! Whirr! Whirr!
This is no shrine of the Things That Were,
But the tingling altar of live To-day,
Where the modern priests of the "Juice" hold sway;
Where the lights are born and the lightnings made
To serve the needs of the world of trade.

Whirr! Whirr! Whirr! Whirr!
The white lights banish the murky blurr,
And over the city, far and near,
The spell extends that was conjured here,
While down in the wheel-pits, far below,
The water whirls in a ceaseless flow—
Foaming and boiling, wild and white,
In a passionate race of tireless might,
Rushing ever the turbines through,
And making the dream, the Dream come true!

Whirr! Whirr! Whirr! Whirr!
The dynamos croon and hum and purr,
And over the city's myriad ways
The jeweled lights all burst ablaze,
And the peak-load comes on the burdened wires
As the folk rush home to their food and fires!

THE POWER PLANT (continued)

Whirr! Whirr! Whirr! Whirr!
This is the heart of the city's stir,
Here where the dynamos croon and sing,
Here where only the "Juice" is King,
Where the switchboard stands in its marble pride,
And the tender watches it, argus-eyed;
Where Death is harnessed and made to serve
By keen-faced masters of brain and nerve;
This is the shrine of the God That Works,
Driving away the mists and murks,
Turning the lightnings into use.
This is the shrine of the mighty "Juice,"
Flowing ever the long wires through,
And making the dream, the Dream come true!

THE WOP

WHEN the line is surveyed through the scenery,
  For tunnel and culvert and cut—
When the contractor has his machinery
  The "big job" is ready—all but—
"All but" means the shovel and pick of it—
  The hunkies who work till they drop.
And so, in the dust and the thick of it,
      Look for the Wop!

The big bosses bear all the fret of it—
  They are the fellows who plan;
But the backbreaking strain and the sweat of it
  Fall to the laboring man—
Dago and Russ and Hungarian—
  All of the immigrant crop.
Where is the job we could carry on—
      Save for the Wop?

Subject for scorn and bedeviling;
  Victim of fraud and chicane—
Still, with his spade he is leveling
  Routes over mountain and plain.
Progress? His soul is the breath of it;
  Lacking his hand, it would stop.
Facing the danger and death of it,
      Here is the Wop!

He knows the toughest and worst of it;
  He knows the hard-driven toil,

[23]

THE WOP (continued)

The ache and the heat and the thirst of it— .
   Never the dream—or the spoil.
Caves and explosions make mud of him—
   Who cares a damn? Let him flop!
Progress is stained with the blood of him—
     Only a Wop!

THE SAND HOG

HE'S fifty inches round the chest,
　His leather lungs are sound,
His heart must stand the air compressed
　In caissons underground;
With pressure hammering his ears,
　His shovel in his hand,
He works—in several atmospheres—
　And burrows in the sand.

Beneath the "lock"
　He spends his time.
He seeks bedrock
　Through silt and slime,
And blithely takes
　His chances where
For us he makes
　A Thoroughfare!

The job would never have a start
　Without the Draughtsman's wit,
The Iron-Worker does his part,
　The Mason adds a bit;
They do their work—remember that—
　But also please recall,
The Sand Hog certainly is at
　The bottom of it all.

THE SAND HOG (continued)

When he is through
   Right on his heel
May come the crew
   With stone and steel;
But till he's done
   They wait their day,
For he's the one
   Who clears the way.

The Engineer says, "Go ahead,"
   The Sand Hog wiggles down,
In tunnels through the river bed,
   Or subways in the town;
Through quicksand, gravel, rock and mud,
   With death itself to dare,
(From falling rock or sudden flood)
   He digs a thoroughfare.

When moisture seeps
   Through chink and crack,
And all that keeps
   The water back
Is air—just air—
   He doesn't shirk,
The job is there—
   And that's his work!

Because he toils and sweats below,
   In steam and dripping heat,
The tall steel buildings rise and throw
   Their shadows on the street.

THE SAND HOG (continued)

    For tubes in which the millions ride
      To do their work each day,
    For bridges flung across the tide,
      The Sand Hog clears the way!

      "A hero"—you
        Would say, perhaps?—
    He's like a slew
        Of other chaps,
    Who only ask
        Their daily pay;
    Who do their task—
        And clear the way!

THE THINKER

BACK of the beating hammer
  By which the steel is wrought,
Back of the workshop's clamor
  The seeker may find the Thought,
The Thought that is ever master
  Of iron and steam and steel,
That rises above disaster
  And tramples it under heel!

The drudge may fret and tinker
  Or labor with dusty blows,
But back of him stands the Thinker,
  The clear-eyed man who Knows;
For into each plow or sabre,
  Each piece and part and whole,
Must go the Brains of Labor,
  Which gives the work a soul!

Back of the motors humming,
  Back of the belts that sing,
Back of the hammers drumming,
  Back of the cranes that swing,
There is the eye which scans them
  Watching through stress and strain,
There is the Mind which plans them—
  Back of the brawn, the Brain!

THE THINKER (continued)

> Might of the roaring boiler,
>   Force of the engine's thrust,
> Strength of the sweating toiler,
>   Greatly in these we trust.
> But back of them stands the Schemer,
>   The Thinker who drives things through;
> Back of the Job—the Dreamer
>   Who's making the dream come true!

THE DEAD REPORTER

HIS typewriter's covered and silent, his chair
    Is empty, his desk is in trim;
It never was so when he used to sit there
    And hammer out "copy" with vim.
The cigarette stubs that he left in a row
    Are gone, and the table is clean,
But give me the mess that the place used to show,
    And the click of his busy machine.

He used to come in with his hat on his ear
    And a limp cigarette on his lip,
With a smile that was crooked, an eye that was clear
    And a tongue that was fluent and flip.
He'd hang up his coat on the hook overhead,
    Tilt his chair to the proper degree,
Run his hands through his hair, which was curly and
      red,
    And write like a cyclone set free.

And sometimes, when pegging away, I forget
    That he isn't one of us still,
And I'll start to say, "Jim, got a good cigarette?"
    And turn toward his battered old "mill,"
And then I'll remember that "30" is in
    For him who once sat in that spot,
And—well, I redouble my hurry and din
    In writing the story I've got.

THE DEAD REPORTER (continued)

His fingers will nevermore clatter the keys,
  His life and his stories are done—
Those stories as brisk as the keen western breeze—
  Another will take up his run.
Another will cover assignments he had.
  He's gone, but the world mustn't lose
Its tales of the sad and the bad and the glad,
  Its regular quota of "news."

A newspaper man's always moving about
  He seldom stays long in a place;
And yet when he leaves, why you haven't a doubt
  That you'll see him again, face to face;
But this—well, it's different, this is the end,
  And the office won't seem just the same.
My "fellow reporter"—and also my friend—
  Is through with the newspaper game.

THE WORKER

I HAVE broken my hands on your granite,
    I have broken my strength on your steel,
I have sweated through years for your pleasure,
    I have worked like a slave for your weal.
And what is the wage you have paid me?
    You masters and drivers of men—
Enough so I come in my hunger
    To beg for more labor again!

I have given my manhood to serve you,
    I have given my gladness and youth;
You have used me, and spent me, and crushed me,
    And thrown me aside without ruth;
You have shut my eyes off from the sunlight,
    My lungs from the untainted air,
You have housed me in horrible places
    Surrounded by squalor and care.

I have built you the world in its beauty,
    I have brought you the glory and spoil,
You have blighted my sons and my daughters,
    You have scourged me again to my toil.
Yet I suffer it all in my patience,
    For somehow I dimly have known
That some day the Worker will conquer
    In a world that was meant for his own!

LEATHER LEGGIN'S

WHIN you want to build a railroad through the
    jungle or the veldt
  Where there's niver anybody bin before,
Why you call on Leather Leggin's, an' he hitches up
    his belt
  An' he takes it as his ordinary chore
To go slashin' through the forests, where the monkeys
    chatter shrill,
  An' the lazy snakes are hissin' down below,
Or to drag a chain an' transit over gulch and grassy
    hill,
  As he marks the route the right-av-way will go!

He's a nervy, wiry divil, with his notebook an' his
    livil,
  An' he doesn't seem to know the name av fear,
He's a sort av scout av Progress, on the payroll as a
    civil—
  (Though he ain't so awful civil, if you say it on the
    livil!)
  On the payroll as a Civil Engineer!

Whin you need to dam a river, or to turn it upside
    down,
  Or to tunnel underneath it in the mud,

[33]

LEATHER LEGGIN'S (continued)

Or to bore an' blast a subway through the innards av
    a town,
  Or to blow aside a mountain with a thud;
When you want to bridge a canyon where there ain't
    no place to cling,
  An' the cliffs is steep an' smoother than a wall,
Why, you call on Leather Leggin's, an' he does that
    little thing,
  An' then comes around an' asks you, "Is that all?"

Oh, he always has a fire in his old an' blackened briar,
  An' he tackles anny job that may appear,
An' he does it on the livil, this here divil of a Civil—
(Though he ain't so very civil, if you put it on the
    livil!)
  This here divil av a Civil Engineer!

Now the bankers down in Wall Street gits the profits
    whin it's done,
  While us heavy-futted diggers gits the can,
But we lifts our hats respectful to the Ingineer, my
    son,
  For that feller, Leather Leggin's, is a Man!
Yes, he takes a heap o' chances, and he works like
    Billy Hell,
  An' his .job is neither peaceable nor tame,
But you bet he knows his business an' he does it
    mighty well,
  An' I want to give him credit for the same!

LEATHER LEGGIN'S (continued)

He is plucky—on the livil—and you'll niver hear him
    snivel,
  Though Fate does her best to put him in the clear,
He's the Grit that niver flinches—on the payroll as a
    Civil,
(For he's sometimes pretty civil, an' he's always on
    the livil!)
  On the payroll as a Civil Engineer!

GRATITUDE

THEY sent me out in the wilderness to build 'em a
      power plant,
Where there wasn't a rail in thirty miles and the trails
      were rough and scant;
They sent me out with a trapper's map, and a husky,
      healthy gang,
That lived and worked from day to day and let all
      else go hang.
There wasn't a sign of a wagon road and the trail was
      a rocky track,
And we had to take machines apart in pieces a mule
      could pack.
So, slow and careful, we hiked along—and gee, what a
      weary tramp,
Till we reached the place I had planned the dam, and
      there we made our camp.

> The sad coyotes howled
>   Like some uncanny choir,
> And bear and wildcat prowled
>   Beyond our sleeping fire,
> But we—in slumber deep,
>   We lay the whole night through,
> For men must get their sleep,
>   When they have work to do.

The ice came down with the winter, the floods came
      down with the spring,

GRATITUDE (continued)

And we fought with that raging river as you fight with
    a living thing.
And we heckled the fat directors, back there in the
    busy town,
For they kept trying to stir us up, while keeping ex-
    penses down.
Whatever supplies we needed, of lumber, cement, or
    steel,
I had to beg and pray for in many a wild appeal.
And while we were bucking nature, in tempest and
    cold and heat,
The fat directors wired me, "Why isn't the job com-
    plete?"

> They'd fume and fuss and fret,
>   And scold and interfere,
> While we—we simply sweat,
>   And tried to keep our cheer.
> In spite of doubt, delay,
>   And fat directors, too,
> We went right on our way,
>   For we had work to do.

They sent me out in the wilderness to build 'em a
    power plant,
And it's running now as it ought to be, though some
    folks said, "It can't!"
And now that everything's smooth and fine, they've
    fastened a can to me,
And they've put in a brand-new graduate, with a nice,
    fresh, school degree.

GRATITUDE (continued)

But say, it was fun while the job was on—a regular
man's size game!—
For we built the dam and power plant, in spite of the
bumps that came;
So the boy is welcome to have the job, and sit in the
office chair—
There's a power plant in the wilderness, and I—I put
it there!

THE FOREST RANGER

I AM sitting here in a ranger's hut in the dusk of the
glimmering gloam,
And I'm trying to make myself think I think I'd rather
be here than home;
And I tell myself of my "wild, free life and the spell
of the forest wide,
With plenty of piney air to breathe and a mighty good
horse to ride."
But somehow I long for a decent house, and the sight
of a polished floor,
And the warm embrace of a leather chair, "as it was
in the days of yore."
No longer they call me a tenderfoot. I reckon I've
met the test,
But I'm longing now for the effete East and not for
the Golden West.

I am sitting here in a ranger's hut, with a bulldog pipe
in my face,
And wishing with all my eager soul for a good cigar
in its place;
And though the suit I am wearing now is the comfiest
sort, I guess,
I wish I were togged in the stiffest kind of conven-
tional evening dress,
With a collar as high as the style allows and a shirt
of vast expanse,

THE FOREST RANGER (continued)

Sitting and smoking as large as life while I waited to get a dance.

Oh, gee! For the sight of the dancing crowd and the sound of a ragtime air,

And the pretty girls with their pretty gowns—and me with the prettiest there!

I am sitting here in a ranger's hut and the tears are in my eyes,

Longing for all of the useless things that city people prize.

I'd like to talk to a fluffy girl with a lot of fluffy chat,

I'd like to eat with seven forks and a bundle of stunts like that.

I know the ways of the forest wild, I can hold my own with men,

But I'm sick to-night for a taste of town and the old fleshpots again.

I reckon the forest would call me back—my woodland paths to roam—

But I'm sitting here in a ranger's hut and wishing that I were home!

READY!

HERE we are, gentlemen; here's the whole gang of
    us,
  Pretty near through with the job we are on;
Size up our work—it will give you the hang of us—
  South to Balboa and north to Colon.
Yes, the canal is our letter of reference;
  Look at Culebra and glance at Gatun;
What can we do for you—got any preference,
  Wireless to Saturn or bridge to the moon?

Don't send us back to a life that is flat again,
  We who have shattered a continent's spine;
Office work—Lord, but we couldn't do that again!
  Haven't you something that's more in our line?
Got any river they say isn't crossable?
  Got any mountains that can't be cut through?
We specialize in the wholly impossible,
  Doing things "nobody ever could do!"

Take a good look at the whole husky crew of us,
  Engineers, doctors and steam-shovel men;
Taken together you'll find quite a few of us
  Soon to be ready for trouble again.
Bronzed by the tropical sun that is blistery,
  Chockful of energy, vigor and tang,
Trained by a task that's the biggest in history,
  Who has a job for this Panama gang?

THE HANDY MAN

SAID Uncle Sam, "I've got a job for some good man
    to do,"
And so he hired an engineer who'd done a thing or
    two;
He gave him money, tools and men and told him, "Go
    ahead!
You cut the continent in two, that's all I ask," he said.
That engineer he fussed and fumed and finally he quit,
And then there came another man who took a whack
    at it;
But still the job was mighty slow—and slower every
    year,
Till Uncle Sam he went and got an Army Engineer.

Now He didn't start in crying
    Of the handicaps he met,
He just set the dirt to flying,
    And the dirt is flying yet!
Handled money by the million
    (But each dollar counted clear),
For he wasn't a civilian,
    But an Army Engineer!

Said Uncle Sam, "I reckon that the boys I teach my-
    self
Are something more than ornaments upon the parlor
    shelf.

THE HANDY MAN (continued)

They may be fond of uniforms when showing on
    parade,
But when they've got a job to do they're worth the
    wages paid.
I show an army man the work and let it go at that,
And when I think of it again the job is finished—pat!
He doesn't ask fool questions and he doesn't sniff and
    sneer,
But he knows his business proper—does the Army
    Engineer!"

      For he isn't playing double,
        And he isn't full of tricks,
      And he keeps himself from trouble
        And from peanut politics.
      There is neither man nor devil
        That can throw him out of gear,
      He is strictly on the level,
        Is the Army Engineer.

Said Uncle Sam, "I reckon if I told him he should try
He would build a bridge of moonbeams from the ocean
    to the sky,
He would tie the worlds together in a harness made
    of light,
And he wouldn't advertise it—but the job would be
    all right!
I don't want to be a boaster, but this army lad of
    mine
Is about the finest ever in his own peculiar line;
He's the kind that you can swear by, he's the kind that
    you can cheer,
He's a quiet peacherino, is the Army Engineer!

THE HANDY MAN (continued)

He is keen and he is canny
  (Grafters call him quite a snob)
And there's no one's got his nanny,
  'Cause he's always on the job.
When the others, all defeated,
  Call the thing a failure sheer,
Why, we get the job completed
  By the Army Engineer!

SONGS OF THE INLAND SEAS

THE REASON

WHENEVER there's a chance to snatch
　　A minute on the sly
I loves to sprawl upon the hatch
　　An' look up at the sky;
It seems so soft an' blue an' deep,
　　With white clouds driftin' slow,
That almost I kin go to sleep
　　With gazin' at it so.

I feels the engine's steady shake
　　Like some big giant's stride,
I hears the combers as they break
　　An' slap against the side;
An' I forgets the fiery pit
　　Where I must work my shift,
An' lies an' simply dreams a bit .
　　An' lets my fancies drift.

I lies there, drowsin' as we plow
　　Acrost the inland sea,
An' kind of thinkin': "Anyhow,
　　There's guys worse off than me.
Fer all the lakes we rides is mine
　　To sail on when I will;
In days of storm er days of shine,
　　When winds is warm er chill."

An' so, away from heat an' soot,
　　I'm happy, after all,

THE REASON (continued)

Till by-an'-by there comes a hoot
An' I'm the guy they call.
An' some one kicks me in the neck
An' swears a streak as well,
An' I must leave the sunny deck
An' go back, down to hell.

ERIE

S HE'S shallow an' muddy an' mean,
    She's chuck full of sandbars an' such,
She's pretty when ca'm an' serene,
    But she's never that way very much.
You hardly kin sail by the chart,
    Her shoals keep a-shiftin' around,
You'll think that you know her by heart,
    When—crunch—an' yer boat is aground!

    She's blowsy an' bleary
      An' nasty—is Erie,
    An' allus just ripe fer a squall,
    She makes us all weary
      An' ugly, does Erie,
    The meanest old lake of them all.

Superior's icy an' rough,
    An' Huron is ugly at times;
Old Michigan's frequently tough,
    But fer faults, misdemeanors an' crimes,
Old Erie—out there in the east—
    Has got 'em all distanced in style.
She's a most undependable beast
    With a temper that's certainly vile.

    You want to be leery
      An' careful of Erie;

ERIE (continued)

> She's husky, although she is small—
> A pugnacious dearie—
> A fighter—is Erie—
> The meanest old lake of them all!

She's choppy an' fickle an' slick;
  One minute she's sweet as a dream,
The next—she'll be makin' you sick
  An' standin' the ship on her beam.
The wind-jammers hates her like sin,
  The steamers is fond of her—not—
She'd ought to be pinched an' run in,
  She's the wickedest one of the lot.

> So don't get too cheery
>   Or flip with Lake Erie,
> She's primed fer a bluff or a brawl,
>   Fer sailin' is skeery
>   An' risky on Erie,
> The meanest old lake of them all!

THE SKIPPER

YOU kin take it from yours truly that I haven't no
      ambition
   For to be the boss an' skipper of a craft,
Though I know there's lots of fellers that considers
      the position
   Is a mighty easy sinecure, a graft.
I know it looks so simple it's a shame to take the
      money—
   That the skipper never seems to do a thing;
But you bet your bottom dollar that the job ain't milk
      an' honey,
   Which is reason for the ditty that I sing.

When the ship is buckin' combers that is threatenin'
      to break her,
   When she's rollin' in the trough or on the ridge,
When the scared an' shakin' wheelsman is a-callin' on
      his Maker,
   An' the waves is throwin' showers on the bridge.
Then the skipper's work is risky, an' it isn't dry an'
      prosy,
   For he's got a ship to handle an' to guide,
While the crew is mostly sheltered in the deck-house
      warm an' cosy,
   An' the wind is makin' trouble far an' wide.

There's a log that must be posted, there's a cargo list
      for keepin',
   There's three thousand tons of freighter on his mind.

THE SKIPPER (continued)

There's the chances he is takin' when the ship is slowly
    creepin'
  Through a fog that makes you feel ye're goin' blind.
There's the bitter winter watches when the bridge is
    frozen solid
  An' the wind is stabbin' at him with a knife,
An' the skipper simply stands it—lookin' satisfied an'
    stolid,
  But I ain't exactly envyin' his life.

An' if the hooker's sinkin', an' the boats is smashed
    an' battered,
  It's the skipper who must be the last to leave;
An' if he bumps a hidden reef his whole career is shat-
    tered
  An' his reputation's gone beyond retrieve.
You can take it from yours truly I don't want to be a
    skipper
  In spite of all the salary he makes,
For I haven't got his worries an' I'm feelin' pretty
    chipper
  As an ordinary seaman on the lakes.

THE MAGIC WHISTLE

I HEARD a steamer whistle at its pier awhile ago,
Heard its giant voice a-quiver, hoarse and deep
and very slow,
Through the window of my office came the rumble
loud and clear,
And it moved me as a song would, some old song I
used to hear.
And I looked up from my writing to the smoky city
skies,
And a misty, hazy vision seemed to form before my
eyes
Of a freighter, heavy loaded, nosing past the harbor
stakes
Like the old "Eulalie" used to when I decked it on
the Lakes.

Every time a steamer whistles with that mighty rum-
bling roar,
It brings back the recollection of the days that are
no more,
When my kit was in my pocket, and I didn't have a
cent,
And the wages of a voyage slowly came and swiftly
went;
When my body was of rubber and of hickory and
steel,
And I knew the way to labor and to put away a meal,

THE MAGIC WHISTLE (continued)

For I didn't live on "health-foods," such as wheat and
    barley flakes,
On the sturdy old "Eulalie," when I decked it on the
    Lakes!

Hear that whistle rumble, rumble like a giant with a
    cold—
Now the old ship's on the junk heap, and I guess I'm
    growing old.
Once my kit was in my pocket—now I travel with a
    trunk;
Now I'm owned by clothes and servants and a lot of
    useless junk,
And I couldn't swing a shovel, lift a hatch or push a
    swab,
And I'm soft and fat and flabby, and I couldn't hold a
    job.
Yet that whistle stirs and thrills me, and my heart it
    aches and aches,
For the sturdy old "Eulalie" when I decked it on the
    Lakes.

THE PACKET BOAT

NEVER no rest,
    Never no sleep,
Say, it would make
    Any Chinaman weep.
Pull outa dock
    Lie down an' snooze—
Land in another, an'
    "No time to lose!"
Hustle the freight out like devils possessed,
Never no sleep, never no rest.

Never no rest,
    Never no sleep,
Say, but they're gettin' us
    Easy an' cheap;
Loadin' all day an'
    Unloadin' all night,
Hittin' the hay
    By the dawn's early light,
Then comes the mate an' we hops from our nest,
Never no sleep, never no rest.

Never no rest,
    Never no sleep,
Stop every port
    An' unload in a heap.
Deckhands we be,
    An' dock wallopers, too,

THE PACKET BOAT (continued)

> Take it from me
> We got plenty to do.
> Finest of packets is bad at the best,
> Never no sleep, never no rest.

> Never no rest,
> Never no sleep,
> Still, we ain't got
> Any protest to peep;
> All we are good fer
> Is pushin' a truck—
> We got the jobs
> An' I guess we're in luck.
> So here's to the packet—the packet be—blessed!
> Never no sleep, never no rest.

THE SIX-HOUR SHIFT
(Coal Passer)

I STARTED in at midnight, I been workin' twenty
    years,
  An' yet the time is only halfpast three;
Above the roarin' boilers the steam gauge sorto sneers,
  As if it was a handin' things to me;
Fer the steam gauge keeps me goin' while the heavin'
    billers roll,
  Keeps me wheelin' to the bunkers mighty swift,
Makes me hurry, hurry, hurry, when the stokers call
    fer coal—
  Why, it seems like sixty hours, this bloomin' shift.

Now, by-and-by the dawn'll break, a sorto sickly gray,
  But I'll be sweatin' here when it has come,
An' if I climb up to the deck to see the peep o' day,
  There'll be a yell, "Hi, get some coal, you bum!"
An' after seven centuries of stewin' here in hell,
  Of shovelin' of fuel by the ton,
Of dumpin' smokin' ashes—why, I hears the breakfast
    bell,
  An' the six-hour shift o' passin' coal is done.

An' if I'm mighty lucky I may get a chanct to sleep
  Till the cookee rings the dinner bell at noon,
An' then I got another shift of six long hours to keep,
  An' of workin' like an overdriven coon;

THE SIX-HOUR SHIFT (continued)

There ain't no time fer dreamin', er fer watchin' of the
lakes—
There ain't no time fer talkin' with the crew,
It's six hours off an' six hours on, no matter how you
aches—
An' the steam gauge allus sneerin' down at you.

THE DOCK WALLOPER

BUFFALO town—an' a cargo to load,
    Boxes an' bales an' such truck to be stowed,
Piled in the warehouses, heaped on the pier,
Looks like a job that would take 'em a year.
Does it? Well, hardly, for soon there's a gang
Ready to stow it, not givin' a hang;
Look at him now, any one of the flock—
Mr. Dock Walloper—there on the dock.

> Good, nervy stock,
> Hard as a rock,
> Strong as a horse, or a tackle an' block,
> Mr. Dock Walloper, there on the dock.

Bossed by a guy that is tough as the rest—
Tougher, I reckon, if put to the test,
Gee, but they tackle that mountain of freight—
Barrel an' bundle, an' basket an' crate.
Truck wheels are squeakin', the tackle-rope sings,
Everyone's cussin' at various things,
Gangways an' trucks an'—well, mostly they knock
Mr. Dock Walloper, there on the dock.

> Good, nervy stock,
> Hard as a rock,
> Strong as a horse, or a tackle an' block,
> Mr. Dock Walloper, there on the dock.

THE DOCK WALLOPER (continued)

Mr. Dock Walloper trots right along,
Doin' his work while his muscles is strong,
Takin' the chances of danger to him,
Gettin' his pay—which is pretty damn slim.
Winches an' clam-shells is hurtin' his trade,
Still, there ain't any machinery made
Quite takes the place of this husky old stock,
Mr. Dock Walloper, there on the dock.

Good, nervy stock,
Hard as a rock,
Strong as a horse, or a tackle an' block,
Mr. Dock Walloper, there on the dock.

SU'GE

(Su'ge is a sort of soft soap—very strong—used in
cleaning deck)

IF you ever got busy with su'ge,
　You know what I'm talkin' about,
Fer I'm worn to a wreck with my scrubbin' the deck
　An' I gotta keep at it, no doubt;
My hands is all crackin' an' peelin',
　My back is fair ready to break,
But I ain't got the gall to take bucket an' all,
　An' chuck 'em kerplunk in the lake.

　　　But su'ge—say, Mister,
　　　　It's steamin' with lye,
　　　Yer hands it'll blister,
　　　　Yer arms it'll fry,
　　　An' when you get through—gee!
　　　　The mate says, "You dub!
　　　Go get some more su'ge,
　　　　More su'ge—an' scrub!"

I know if they took all the su'ge
　I used since I got on this boat,
An' measured the stuff, they'd have more than
　　enough
　To keep a whole navy afloat.
My grub is all tastin' of su'ge,
　My pipe smells all day of the dope;
An' when I'm asleep I imagine I'm deep
　In a kettle of su'ge an' soap.

SU'GE (continued)

Fer su'ge is slimy
 An' stronger each day.
It allus is by me—
 I can't get away.
I never get through. Gee!
 I scrape an' I rub,
An' then get more su'ge,
 More su'ge an' scrub!

I ain't got no pictures of Heaven,
 But this I will firmly declare:
If Heaven's a place where the deckhands have space,
 There isn't no su'ge up there.
But hell must be chuck full of su'ge,
 With millions of corners to swab,
An' if I should go to that country below,
 I sure would be trained fer the job.

But su'ge I'm hatin'
 Much worser than jail,
An' just fer that, Satan
 Would hand me a pail
An' say, "Oh, I knew'd ye,
 Ye commonplace dub,
So here's some more su'ge;
 Get busy—an' scrub!"

CHRISTMAS ON THE GREAT LAKES

DECK is just a slab of ice, gunnels plastered white,
    Every stay is covered thick with a winter coat;
Christmas! But the whistlin' wind's bitter cold to-
    night,
    Glad I'm not the guy up there pilotin' the boat.
Hear them combers slap the bow; bet the flyin' spray
    Freezes on his overcoat, as his watch he takes.
Hark, the siren's screamin' out in her fiendish way,
    Gee, but it's a happy time, Christmas on the Lakes!

Engines throbbin' steadily, faithful-like an' true,
    Stoke-hole's just as blazin' hot as it ever were;
Got to keep the gauges up, got to "push her through,"
    Christmas can't delay the boat, what's the day to
    her?
"Merry Christmas," grins the mate, when his face he
    shows,
    Yellin' to us on the decks, as the mornin' breaks,
Then he calls us all the things that his fancy knows,
    That's the way the day begins—Christmas on the
    Lakes.

Cook he boils a hen or so, makes some special pie,
    Maybe gives us puddin', too, like we got at home.
(What you kind of winkin' at—smoke is in yer eye?
    You ain't even *written* back since you "hit the
    foam.")

CHRISTMAS ON THE GREAT LAKES (continued)

We ain't got no sentiments, guys like you an' me,
    We ain't ever blue an' sad—lonesome till we aches—
We ain't wishin' we was home, round the Christmas
        tree—
    Naw, we love a night like this, Christmas on the
        Lakes.

Deck is just a slab of ice, wind is shriekin' shrill,
    Foc'sl's full of smoke an' dust, hot an' close an' foul.
Yet it's kind of different, everybody's still,
    No one ain't a-sayin' much—hear that siren howl.
Maybe they're just petered out fightin' wet an' sleet,
    Maybe they are dreamin' dreams such as mem'ry
        wakes,
(Hear the combers crash an' smash, feel the engines
        beat)
Ninety miles from Mackinac—Christmas on the
        Lakes.

L'ENVOI

WHEN I've finished my final voyage an' taken my
latest breath,
An' gone to the strange new harbor ye're landed in
after death,
I want shore leave fer a while er so in the city of the
blest.
(Providin' that is the port I hit, an' I'm hopin' fer the
best.)
An' then, with a brand-new outfit, I'll climb back over
the side,
An' sail away on a good long trip acrost the heavenly
tide
With a mate that knows his business, a competent
engineer—
An' me? I'll be a deckhand, the same as I am down
here.

But the work'll be dead easy, an' most of the time I'll
lie
Propped up on a comfy hatch-top, a-watchin' the
clouds go by,
With the steady engines beatin' an' keepin' a lively
pace,
An' the wind of the open water a-blowin' across my
face,
An' the cook'll ring fer dinner, an' we'll all come
troopin' in,
To a meal that would fill you with joy an' bliss an'
make a dyspeptic grin;

L'ENVOI (continued)

An' after it's done we kin set an' smoke while the good
    ship drives ahead,
An' thank our stars that we ain't alive, but only happy
    an' dead.

The pay will be all we've wanted, the quarters bet-
    ter'n we dream,
We'll touch at ports like the Isles of Bliss, where the
    lights is all agleam;
Fer I know I wouldn't be happy a-spendin' my time on
    land,
Not even there in Heaven, on the beautiful golden
    strand.
So I think the Lord will fix it so sailor men can sail
On lakes or seas like they used to, a bravin' the storm
    an' gale;
Fer, as Mr. Kipling puts it, we wouldn't know what
    to do
Without no seas where we could live the only life we
    knew.

SONGS OF DEEPWATER

THE IMPULSE

YER crew may come from the dregs of town,
    Kicked an' beaten an' hammered down,
But show 'em how an' drive 'em hard,
An' they'll carry you through to harbor, pard;
They'll work like fiends of the workin' kind,
An' they'll follow you anywhere, follow blind;
They'll brave a storm in a peanut shell,
If the pay is good an' you feed 'em well.

They'll cling to the icy decks and fight
The storm an' the sleet an' the snow all night;
They'll patch the leaks an' they'll mend the sails,
They'll take a chance with the toughest gales,
They'll man the pumps through a hurricane,
An' laugh an' joke as the rivets strain,
In the mighty rush of the heavin' swell,
If you pay 'em good an' you feed 'em well.

They'll shovel yer coal in the fire-hole deep,
They'll work long shifts with little sleep,
They'll lash 'emselves to the whirlin' wheel
While the deck's a-wash an' the lanterns reel,
They'll stand the drenchin' of frigid waves,
They'll swear like truckmen an' toil like slaves,
They'll jump to the job at yer quickest yell,
If you pay 'em good an' you feed 'em well.

But the best old crew that kin be had
Ain't worth a cent if the chuck is bad;

THE IMPULSE (continued)

They'll growl an' grumble an' shirk an' grunt,
They'll bungle over the simplest stunt;
But give 'em the grub an' the proper pay,
And they'll sail you anywhere, anyway,
They'd steer you safe through the fires of hell,
If you paid 'em good an' you fed 'em well.

THE WINDJAMMER

THE sailin' ship's full of the greatest romance"—
　　You'll read that somewhere in a book.
Romantic?　Why, say, Jack, she hasn't a chance—
　　She looks like a frowsy old cook;
Her sails is all patched like a old pair of pants,
　　An' *that* don't express how they look.
She's gen'rally snubnosed an' lackin' of paint—
She's useful, all right; but romantic she ain't.

Say, the guy that would want to put her in a song
　　Would call a plain schooner a brig;
You'll see her go rootin' an' crawlin' along
　　With about as much grace as a pig,
Or a drunken old fishwoman goin' it strong
　　An' tappin' each bar fer a swig.
You can't say she's handsome er noble er quaint—
She's useful, all right; but romantic she ain't.

Her decks are awash an' there's lumber on top.
　　She squatters along like a duck,
An' she "bams!" through the waves with an awkward
　　　　"kerflop!"
　　An' she grunts at the waves she has struck—
She acts like a crazy old dame with a mop
　　That splashes around in the muck,
An' sometimes the smell of her'd make you grow faint,
She's useful, all right; but romantic she ain't.

THE WINDJAMMER (continued)

When swamped she will cheerfully settle—an' ride,
  Held up by the lumber she totes,
While the crew an' the captain sit up on the side
  Just tickled to death that she floats;
She hasn't no grace an' she hasn't no pride—
  She's a kind of a hobo of boats.
She hasn't much manners, er sense, er restraint—
She's useful, all right; but romantic she ain't.

So take it from me—as I've asked you before—
  The windjammer's nothin' so strange.
Poetic? Perhaps—like a general store
  Er the nigger cook's new galley range;
I worked on one once—but I won't any more;
  It gave me the scurvy—an' mange.
You take it from me, though I hain't no complaint—
She's useful, all right; but romantic?—she ain't.

THE STOKER

WAY down below the lower deck an' just above the
keel
Our stoke-hole crew they tramps around on hard and
smokin' steel,
Right in a glare that makes you blind, a heat that
makes you reel,
    We feeds the blazin' boilers day an' night,
We're red of eye an' black with coal, an' though the
shift is short,
The sweat of workin' in that hell is measured by the
quart;
This stokin' liners' boilers ain't no mollycoddle sport,
    But we gotta keep the boat a-goin' right.

    It's shovel, shovel, shovel!
      An' it's sweat, sweat, sweat!
    With the heat a-whoopin' round you
      An' yer hull frame wet;
    With the cinders all a-droppin'
      An' the grates a-roar,
    As they seem to yell for fuel,
      Sayin', "More! More! More!"

The Captain on the windy bridge is something grand
to see,
An' the Engineer's a personage as great as he can be,
But the tub would never travel if it weren't fer mugs
like me,
    The guys you never know is on the ship.

THE STOKER (continued)

If we didn't keep on stokin' spite of all the sweat an'
    stew,
If we didn't feed the boilers, what the devil would
    they do?
There wouldn't be no power for to turn the bloomin'
    screw,
    An' there wouldn't be no record-breakin' trip!

    It's shovel, shovel, shovel!
      An' it's sweat, sweat, sweat!
    We're tryin' to cut the record
      An' we'll do it yet,
    While the draft would almost suck you
      Through the furnace door,
    An' the hungry grates is callin',
      "Give us more, more, more!"

They packs us down in quarters that a Chink would
    hardly bear,
An' now an' then they condescends to let us breathe
    the air
(When the passengers ain't lookin' an' there ain't a
    soul to care;)
    So we sweats our lives in the service to the Line,
And the prize for all our labors is a mighty little pay,
An' a bunch of rotten vittles that 'ud make you faint
    away,
An' the end is very simple—there's a little splash of
    spray,
    An' another stoker's buried in the brine!

THE STOKER (continued)

It's shovel, shovel, shovel!
An' it's sweat, sweat, sweat!
It ain't no merry picnic,
You can make that bet;
But we gotta keep the pressure
While the hot grates roar,
Their everlastin' holler,
"Give us more! more! more!"

THE PEACEABLE MIN

FAHEY, Mulcahey, McCann,
   Dooley, Gilhooley an' Flynn,
Each wan a good Irish man,
   All of thim peaceable min,
Got off the ship fer a stroll,
   Wint in a bar for a dhrink,
Each of thim flashin' a roll
   Makin' the bartendher blink.

Prisintly gathered a gang—
   Gang that was certainly tough,
Rowin' around the shebang,
   Cuttin' up ugly an' rough;
Twinty-five min at the least
   Hovered around fer to rob,
Plannin' a spree an' a feast,
   Whin they had finished the job.

Somebody started a fight,
   Somebody pulled out a knife,
Trouble was surely in sight,
   There was a row fer yer life;
Guns all a-wavin' in air,
   Shots an' a smother av smoke,
Manny an uplifted chair,
   Manny a cranium broke.

Fahey, Mulcahey, McCann,
   Dooley, Gilhooley and Flynn,

THE PEACEABLE MIN (continued)

Each wan a peaceable man,
  Each av thim unarmed min,
Did just the best that they could,
  Fightin' their way to the door.
Bar was a sphlinter av wood,
  Glass scattered over the floor.

Prisintly all things was sthill,
  Sthill as a village asleep,
Thim who had stharted the mill
  Lyin' around in a heap,
Out av that dump came the clan,
  Smilin' as whin they came in,
Fahey, Mulcahey, McCann,
  Dooley, Gilhooley an' Flynn!

FOG

WHEN the fog-horn blows
    With its "Hoo-oo! Hoo-oo! Hoo-oo!"
Then the old tub's nose
    Just goes pokin' through,
Where the fog hangs thick
    An' the water's gray,
An' it's no cinch trick
    Fer to find yer way,
An' it's slo-ow she goes,
When the fog-horn blows!

When the fog-horn blows
    With its "Hoo-oo! Hoo-oo! Hoo-oo!"
Do you suppose
You kin snooze er doze?
No—that fog-horn deep
    Hoots the hull shift long,
An' it spoils yer sleep
    With its hoarse, bass song;
You kin bet you knows
When the fog-horn blows.

When the fog-horn blows,
    With its "Hoo-oo! Hoo-oo! Hoo-oo!"
Each deck light grows
    Kind of dim to you,
Kind of sick an' pale,
An' the air feels stale,

FOG (continued)

> An' yer heart sinks low,
>   An' you hears the screw
> Turnin' over—slo-ow—
> Fer it's slo-ow she goes
> When the fog-horn blows!
>
> When the fog-horn blows
>   Why, yer ship must crawl,
> Where the compass shows;
>   An' you prays—that's all,
> As along you slide
>   In the fog an' dark,
> That you don't collide
>   With another—Hark!
> There's a ship, "Hoo-oo! Hoo-oo!"
> 'Twas her fog-horn blew!
> Yes, it's "Hoo-oo! Hoo-oo! Hoo-oo!"
> "Look out, hoo-oo! Hoo-oo!"
> It's so you goes
> When the fog-horn blows!

REPARTEE

SAYS the Captain of the tugboat to the skipper of
the barge,
"I hain't anything against you, but, to take you by an'
large,
Ye're a fuzzy-nosed gorilla that is always crazy drunk,
An' you otta be a-runnin' of a store fer sellin' junk.
Ye're a lubber that is cross-eyed, an' yer brain is buck-
wheat cakes,
An' I guess the way you got here—someone wished
you on the Lakes—
If they sold you fer a nickel it would be an over-
charge,"
Says the Captain of the tugboat to the skipper of the
barge.

Says the skipper of the coal barge to the Captain of
the tug,
"There's a padded cell awaitin' fer your special kind of
bug,
I ain't got a thing ag'in you—'cept the color of yer
hair,
An' yer looks an' ways an' actions an' the kind of
clothes you wear;
I'm just kinda *SORRY* fer you—fer your temper an'
yer shape—
As a human ye're a failure, but you'd make a hand-
some ape.

REPARTEE (continued)

I would git a job as wild man if I had yer awful mug,"
Says the skipper of the coal-barge to the Captain of
the tug.

Then the Captain of the tugboat climbed upon the coal-
barge deck,
An' the skipper of the coal-barge fell upon his brawny
neck,
An' they wrastled an' they pounded an' they shouted
an' they swore,
An' it looked—the way they acted—they was out fer
blood an' gore.
Says the Captain of the tugboat, "Well, it's good to
meet you here."
Says the skipper of the coal-barge, "Same to you, Bill,
have a beer?"
An' the two old pals an' cronies—arm in arm they goes
below,
Fer 'twas just to show affection that they cussed each
other so!

WESTERN BALLADS

THE HILLS

PARTNER, remember the hills?
The gray, barren, bleak old hills,
We knew so well—
Not these gentle, placid slopes that swell
In lazy undulations, lush and green.
No; the real hills, the jagged crests,
The sharp and sheer-cut pinnacles of earth
That stand against the azure—gaunt, serene,
Careless of all our little worsts and bests,
Our sorrow and our mirth!

Partner, remember the hills?
Those snow-crowned, granite battlements of hills
We loved of old.
They stood so calm, inscrutable and cold,
Somehow it never seemed they cared at all
For you or me, our fortune or our fall,
And yet we felt their thrall;
And ever and forever to the end
We shall not cease, my friend,
To hear their call.

Partner, remember the hills?
The grim and massive majesty of hills
That soared so far,
Seeming, at night, to scrape against a star.
Do you remember how we lay at night
(When the great herd had settled down to sleep)
And watched the moonshine—white

THE HILLS (continued)

Against the peaks all garlanded with snow,
While soft and low
The night wind murmured in our ears—and so
We wrapped our blankets closer, looked again
At those great, shadowy mountaintops, and then
Sank gently to our deep
And quiet sleep?

Partner, remember the hills?
The real hills, the true hills.
Ah, I have tried
To brush the memory of them aside;
To learn to love
These fresh, green hills the poets carol of;
But the old gray hills of barrenness still hold
My heart so much in thrall
That I forget the beauty all about,
The grass and flowers and all;
And just cry out
To take again the faint and wind-swept trail,
To see my naked mountains, shale and snow,
To feel again the hill-wind and to know
The spell that shall not fail.

NOSTALGIA

I 'M goin' home where the mountains are,
   Where a man's own eyes kin see as far
And farther too—in that atmosphere—
Than a man with a telescope kin here.

I'm goin' home to the minin' town,
Where the boys is sinkin' the deep shafts down;
Where the hills is steep an' the scenery's bare,
An' there ain't no foliage anywhere—
      I'm goin' home.

I'm goin' home to the raw old camp,
Where the whistles hoot an' the engines stamp;
Where nobody asks you, "Who are you?"
But only, "Hey there; what kin you do?"
Where the slag dumps glow an' the ore cars bang,
An' the six-horse teamsters shout, "G'lang!"
Where the chimneys flare with a hundred hues;
Where you play the game with a stack of blues,
Whoop if you're winner an' grin if you lose;
Where the pace is fast an' the blood runs hot,
An' you blow in all of the cash you've got—
      I'm goin' home.

I'm goin' home to my own again,
To the breezy girls an' the six-foot men,
To the rocky hills an' the sagebrush plains,
Where it always pours an' it never rains;

NOSTALGIA (continued)

Six thousand feet above the sea,
Where the heart beats swift an' the soul is free;
Where you live like a live one—an' when you die
They lay you under the alkali
An' drink to your soul in a whisky straight,
An' shake fer the drinks at the graveyard gate.
You kin have my job an' my office space;
I want to get out to the good old place
Where the peaks are white as the ocean foam—
        I'm goin' home.

THE EXILE

I WANT to go, want to go, want to go west again,
  Back where the men are the biggest and best
    again,
Back where my life will have savor and zest again,
  Gee, but I'm sick for it, sick for it all;
Sick to go back where my heart is unbound again,
Somehow I'm lost and I want to be found again
Where I belong, on my natural ground again,
  Up where the men and the mountains are tall.

I want to go, want to go, want to go west again,
Wing myself back like a bird to the nest again
Feel the free air in my throat and my chest again,
  Up where it's roomy and open and grand;
Up where the sunshine is golden and glorious,
Manners as bluff and as breezy as Boreas,
Nobody distant—and no one censorious,
  Comradeship sure of the deep western brand.

I want to go, want to go, want to go west again!
Hear the old gang with its quip and its jest again,
Ride a good horse and be decently dressed again
  (Corduroys, stetson and old flannel shirt!)
Flowers and trees? I have suffered a blight of them,
Give me the peaks with the gray and the white of them,
(Granite and snow) I am sick for the sight of them,
  —Blessed old memories, yet how they hurt!

THE EXILE (continued)

I want to go, want to go, want to go west again,
Put all my dreams of the past to the test again,
(Gorges and canyons and cliffs and the rest again
   Heaving themselves in their grandeur to view;)
Let me but feel the old thrill in my breast again,
Know camaraderie mutely expressed again,
Gee, but I want to go, want to go west again,
   Back to the Mountains, old Girl, and to YOU!

THE FANCY SHOTS

(Incident taken in part from a story by Emerson
Hough)

THEY come in town a-whoopin' an' they raised
a-plenty hell,
They was bold and wicked bad men an' they ran things
for a spell.
They was shootin' round promiscus like a Wild West
Show parade,
They had everybody duckin', they had everyone
afraid;
When they saw the city marshal, in his hat they shot a
hole,
Then they had him nimbly dancin' while they done
the double roll;
They could keep a tin can rollin' with the bullets from
a gun,
An' the stunts they didn't show us simply never had
been done.

But at last they both departed, havin' nearly wrecked
the town,
An' the sheriff came in after—on his face a worried
frown,
An' he says some cattle rustlers has been busy round
of late,
An' he gives us their descriptions—it was Them, as
sure as Fate!

THE FANCY SHOTS (continued)

So we told him of their shootin', of their quickness an'
    their skill,
An' we says they sure would git him if they really shot
    to kill,
For the sheriff ain't no wonder, just an ordinary shot,
Though the people he went after he most generally
    got!
When we offered him a posse, he just grinned and
    shook his head.
"You kin hitch me up a wagon an' I'll go alone," he
    said.
"I ain't got no shootin' irons but this rifle here of
    mine,
There's a couple bullets in it, just as good as eight or
    nine—
I ain't much on fancy motions, bustin' crystal balls an'
    such,
But I wants them cattle rustlers, an' I wants 'em very
    much."

Well, we hitches up the wagon an' we says to him,
    "Good-bye,"
An' most every feller present had some moisture in
    his eye,
Fer we kind of likes that sheriff, an' we hates to see
    him die!
But he drives away a-hummin' of a funny kind of
    tune,
An' we all goes back to drinkin' in the Yellow Dog
    Saloon.

THE FANCY SHOTS (continued)

Now there ain't no twists an' turnin's to this here
veracious tale,
In half a day or sooner we see something on the
trail,
An' at last the dust cloud parted, an' we makes it
plainly then—
It's the sheriff on his wagon, drivin' calmly home
again.
He is whistlin' soft an' tender on that same fool melody,
An' he wasn't none excited far as anyone could see,
But underneath the canvas on that little wagon floor
Was them two bad cattle rustlers that would never
rustle more.

I don't know the way he done it, but the moral's plain
an' clear,
You may shoot tin cans an' quarters tossed up in the
atmosphere,
You may make the natives wonder at yer marvelous
control,
You may break the shootin' records, do the nifty
double roll,
But the really fancy shooter, when you git right down
to pan,
Is the guy who pulls the quickest an' who always gits
his man!

AND HALLOWELL CHAWED

SAYS Bill the Bad'un, as he blows in:
 "You've heard 'em tell of Original Sin?"
Well, I'm that party—the toughest yet;
The sort of person who'd just as soon
Shoot up the gang in a bum saloon
As scratch a match fer a cigarette."
Then he shoots the glasses offen the bar
An' the gang it ducks—fer it looks like war;
Yet Hallowell never stops his jaws
As he chaws an' chaws an' chaws an' chaws.

Says Bill the Bad'un: "Say, I'm the worst
That ever carried a man's-size thirst.
There's a private buryin'-ground I've got,
A quiet an' peaceful an' lonesome spot;
An' though it's crowded a bit, I think
It could hold a dozen as like as not
If I planted you close in that little plot—
Will somebody kindly purchase a drink?"—
Hallowell doesn't stop ner pause
But chaws an' chaws an' chaws an' chaws.

The tremblin' barkeeper sets 'em up,
An' Bill the Bad'un he waves his Krupp
An' orders the crowd that's left to prance
In a pained an' ponderous sort of dance.
But it don't quite meet with Bill's applause,
Fer Hallowell still just sets an' chaws.

AND HALLOWELL CHAWED (continued)

Says Bill the Bad'un: "There's one old gent
Who doesn't appear to know what's meant
By the terpsichorean art I teach—
I'll briefly explain in a louder speech."
So a shot rang out and another, too,
An' the county coroner hove in view.

Now down in that private buryin'-ground
Is a heap of earth in a six-foot mound;
An' often you'll notice, a-settin' there,
A quiet man with a languid air,
Who says, with barely an eyelash flicker:
"There's some is quick an' others is quicker,
But those that's quick is frequent dead
An' those that's quicker is quick instead."
An' havin' expounded these simple laws,
Hallowell chaws an' chaws an' chaws.

THE PROSPECTOR

MY pick is stuck in my belt loop, my pipe is stuck
   in my face,
I'm off to the snowy mountains, I'm moving from place
   to place,
With the clear, cool air about me and the chance for a
   "strike" ahead
And all of my cares and troubles back in the town I've
   fled.
Smoking my strong tobacco, humming my happy song,
I'm off on the search for the gold I have hoped, the
   gold I have sought so long;
But whether I find it, or fail again, whatever my fate
   deems best,
At least I'll have been on the hike once more and
   sated my wild unrest.

Sometimes with no walls around me, no roof but the
   sky above,
I lie in my army blankets and—ponder on life and
   love?
Well, no, I puff on my briar, I'm held by the night in
   thrall,
And I watch the thin smoke melt away and think of
   nothing at all.
Peace to the wide world's worries, they are millions of
   miles afar.
They look as tiny and dim to me as the uttermost tiny
   star—

THE PROSPECTOR (continued)

And the nightwind brushes my temples, and drowsy
visions creep
Into my idle, care-free brain and then comes a dream-
less sleep.

My pick is stuck in my belt loop, my pipe is stuck in
my face,
I'm off on another prospect hoping that I may trace
Some vein of the yellow metal, or even the red or
white,
And never was heart more hopeful and never were
hopes more bright.
What if I never strike it? You ask with a pitying
smile.
Why, friend, the very searching is many times worth
the while,
For it lifts my troubles from me, and I know from the
very start
That one sort of gold I am sure to gain, the gold of a
carefree heart.

PARDNERS

(The Cowpuncher to His Pony)

YOU bad-eyed, tough-mouthed son-of-a-gun,
　Ye're a hard little beast to break,
But ye're good fer the fiercest kind of run
　An' ye're quick as a rattlesnake.
You jolted me good when first we met,
　In the dust of the bare corral,
An' neither one of us will ferget
　The fight that we fit, old pal.

But now—well, say, old hoss, if John
　D. Rockefeller shud come
With all of the riches his paws are on
　An' want to buy you, you bum,
I'd laugh in his face an' pat yer neck,
　An' say to him loud an' strong,
"I wouldn't sell you this durned old wreck
　Fer all of yer cash—so long!"

Fer we have slept on the barren plains,
　An' cuddled against the cold,
We've been through tempests of drivin' rains
　When the heaviest thunder rolled;
We've raced with fire on the "lone prairee,"
　An' run from the mad stampede;
An' there ain't no money can buy from me
　A pard of yer style an' breed.

PARDNERS (continued)

    So I reckon we'll stick together, pard,
      Till one of us cashes in.
    Ye're wiry an' tough an' mighty hard,
      An' homlier, too, than sin;
    But yer head's all there an' yer heart's all right,
      An' you've been a good pardner, too.
    An' if you've a soul it's clean and white—
      You ugly old scoundrel, you!

THE THRALL OF THE GOLDEN GATE

IT'S mighty far to Frisco town,
  Where streets run steeply up and down,
It's over all a continent, and I am busted, too.
  Yet I am sick for Kearney Street,
  Where all the old tramps royal meet,
And I am going back again to join that royal crew!

Yes, it is far to Frisco town, to Frisco town, to Frisco
    town,
  But I will get there, hook or crook, there always is a
    way!
I'll hit the trail for Frisco town, for fair old, rare old
    Frisco town,
  That lies so happy on her hills and looks upon the
    bay!

Oh, hearts were light in Frisco town,
  That loves to laugh and hates to frown,
(I laughed my share when I was there so many years
    ago)
  But though she's burnt and built again
  And strange to such as loved her then,
I'm going back to Frisco town, the town I used to
    know!

Yes, it is far to Frisco town, to Frisco town, to Frisco
    town,
  But I would rather beg or starve beside the Golden
    Gate,

THE THRALL OF THE GOLDEN GATE (continued)

And be again in Frisco town, in dear old, queer old
    Frisco town,
  Than have a million dollars here and live in gaudy
    state!

  The girls are fair in Frisco town
  And each one wears her gayest gown
(And O the glory of their eyes from inky black to
    gray!)
  I wonder if there's still displayed
  The bright and brilliant dress parade
That used to float along the line just after matinée!

It's far, it's far to Frisco town, to Frisco town, to
    Frisco town,
  But though I have to beat my way I'm game to make
    the trip
To smiling, wiling Frisco town, to Frisco town, to
    Frisco town,
  Where life was like a dry champagne that tingles on
    the lip!

  Oh, time goes swift in Frisco town,
  Where fortune bobs you up and down,
Where no one counts to-morrow till to-morrow is to-
    day!
  The city glorious and glad,
  The city—everything but sad!
The city full of lights and love, and never less than
    gay!

THE THRALL OF THE GOLDEN GATE (continued)

It's mighty far to Frisco town, to Frisco town, to
    Frisco town,
    (But O the lights that used to shine from wine shop
      and café!)
I'll hit the trail to Frisco town, to light old, bright old
    Frisco town,
    That lies so happy on her hills and looks upon the
      bay!

THE COWARD

SAYS Alkali Ike, "Though it may be true
   That bad men's eyes is a quiet blue,
An' their hands is small an' their voices low,
An' I got all of them marks to show,
Yet I hereby claim, depose an' state,
Reckon, declare an' kalkilate,
That I am the peacefulest person here—
I says it loud an' I says it clear,
I'm the quietest, kindest, meekest guy
That ever was seen by the human eye."

Says Alkali Ike, as he drunk a drink,
"Honestly, boys, I'm the ca'mest gink,
With the softest heart an' the kindest ways
Of any feller you'll meet these days.
I preaches peace an' I lives it—right,
I ain't no hand fer a scrap er fight,
I'm so slow to anger there's folks who claim
That I got no honor er sense of shame,
They sees me lettin' things go so far
They reckon I'm cowardly——"
                                  "And you are,"
Says the stranger, leanin' acrost the bar,
An' everyone ducks, fer it looks like war.

"I am!" says Ike, as he draws his gat,
"Well, mebbe I am, but I won't take that!"
"G'wan," says the stranger; "chuck it, scat!

[103]

THE COWARD (continued)

I ain't no bad man, I got no gun,
Go on an' shoot—when the job is done
They'll tell how yer brave young heart was steeled
To puncture a feller—that wasn't heeled."

Says Alkali Ike, "Why, durn my eyes,
Ye're dead right, friend; I apologize."
Then he peeled his coat an' his cartridge belt,
An' he took off his guns an' his Stetson felt,
An' he says, "Though a person of peace I am,
I'll fight you, stranger, yer own way,"—Bam!
An' he hit that guy on his ugly chin,
An' the stranger fell in a heap—all in.

Says Alkali Ike, "You have often heard
Of the Dove of Peace—well, I'm that bird.
Is there any doubt of the fact? What? No?
All right, let's licker, here's to you, bo!"

PLAYING THE GAME

YES, he went an' stole our steers,
    So, of course, he had to die;
I ain't sheddin' any tears,
    But, when I cash in—say, I
    Want to take it like that guy—
Laughin', jokin' with the rest,
    Not a whimper, not a cry,
Standin' up to meet the test
    Till we swung him clear an' high,
With his face turned toward the west!

Here's the way it looks to me;
Cattle thief's no thing to be,
But, if you take up that trade,
Be the best one ever made;
If you've got a thing to do
Do it strong an' SEE IT THROUGH!

That was him! He played the game,
    Took his chances, bet his hand,
When at last the showdown came
    An' he lost, he kept his sand;
Didn't weep an' didn't pray,
    Didn't waver er repent,
Simply tossed his cards away,
    Knowin' well just what it meant.
Never claimed the deck was stacked,
    Never called the game a snide,

PLAYING THE GAME (continued)

> Acted like a man should act,
>   Took his medicine—an' died!
>
> So I say it here again,
> What I think is true of men;
> They should try to do what's right,
> Fair an' square an' clean an' white,
> But, whatever is their line,
> Bad er good er foul er fine,
> Let 'em go the Limit, play
> Like a plunger, that's the way!

THE SUNSET TRAIL

OUT along the sunset trail
    Life was never dull or stale;
You could allus take a chance,
Where the mountains reached so far
Knockin' up ag'in a star!
Seems as if I *had* to go
When the past is callin' so,
Got to answer to the hail
From the pals I used to know
Out along the sunset trail!

Out along the sunset trail
Life was something new an' glad,
There weren't no distinctions pale—
Good was good an' bad was bad—
(Bad was extry double bad!)
There was women there an' men
Like we'll never see again,
Swaggerin' an' quick an' proud,
Loyal, laughin', rough an' loud,
Buckin' any game they played
Like they thought they couldn't fail.
They weren't pikers, er afraid,
Out along the sunset trail!

Out along the sunset trail
Life was swift an' blood was red.

THE SUNSET TRAIL (continued)

Now them flamin' days is dead,
Things is quiet-like an' pale.
Yet I reckon if it came
To a p'int where there was need,
They could play the same old game,
Play it with the same old speed,
They could fight an' work an' love,
Like the folk I'm singin' of;
Women still are women—brave,
Kind an' tender, to the grave,
Men are big an' true an'—Male!
Out along the sunset trail!

SONGS OF THE COPPER COUNTRY

THE SMOKE-EATER

HE stands in the middle of Hell an' grins,
　　Where a salamander would choke,
His hide's constructed of elephant skins,
　　His diet is sulphur smoke.
The throat of the brute is black as black,
　　An' his lungs is a similar shade,
An' he hasn't a shirt to his sweatin' back,
　　When he's swelterin' at his trade.

　　　　Eatin' the smoke,
　　　　Eatin' the smoke,
　　　　　Eatin' the smoke with vim.
　　　　Sometimes I kick
　　　　At my own hard trick—
　　　　　But I wouldn't trade jobs with him.

Where the long blast furnaces snort an' roar,
　　Or the calcine tables turn,
Or out on the big converter floor
　　He has his livin' to earn.
An' all he does is to play with fire
　　The whole of the workin' day,
An' breathe hot smoke to his heart's desire
　　As long as he draws his pay.

　　　　Eatin' the smoke,
　　　　Eatin' the smoke,
　　　　　Watchin' the hot matte glare.

THE SMOKE-EATER (continued)

> You wouldn't pine
> For a job like mine—
>   But it's better than that one there.

He tramps around in arsenic dust,
  In a sort of inferno scene;
With slag-pots sputterin' fit to bust
  An' molten copper that's green.
Copper that's green an' blue an' red
  As it boils when the blast whoops through,
An' big cranes swingin' above his head
  With caldrons of molten stew.

> Eatin' the smoke,
> Eatin' the smoke,
>   That's what a man is fer.
> It's the same old song,
> Of a whole life long—
>   "Fer the sake of the kids an' Her!"

THE MINER

THE old prospector he finds the claim,
   The young surveyor he marks the same,
And the carpenter builds the gallows frame,
   And the teamster he hauls the coal;
The foreman tells 'em the way to do,
   The engineer hoists a cage or two,
But listen to this, I'm a-tellin' you—
   It's the Miner who digs the hole!

     Colonel—another bowl!
     I'm dry as a roasted soul,
       I've had to choke
       On powder smoke,
     My teeth are full of the rock I've broke,
     For I am one poor son-of-a-gun—
       A Miner who digs the hole!

He must work in gas and see in the dark,
The music he hears is the air-drill's bark,
It isn't no "picnic in the park,"
   It isn't no cinch he's stole;
He's carpenter, plumber, machinist—yes,
A sort of surveyor, too, I guess—
A little of everything—more or less,
   The Miner who digs the hole!

     Colonel—another bowl!
     I'm fat with my pay-day roll,

THE MINER (continued)

> With rent and such
> It ain't so much,
> But I'm glad I'm walkin' without a
>   crutch!
> For I am one poor son-of-a-gun,
> A Miner who digs the hole!

There's the fire to fight and the miner's con,
Rickety ladders to step upon,
A missed hole found—and a miner gone,
   And you'll hear the church bells toll;
But hell!—we've got to "make her pay!"
And we get our three and a half a day,
So have another on me, I say!
   You Miners who dig the hole!

> Colonel—another bowl!
> Heaven's our final goal!
>   The mines are hot
>   But they're all we've got,
> And they'll last awhile, as like as not,
> And we are the ones—poor sons-of-guns,
>   The Miners who dig the hole!

THE TEAMSTER

WITH a five-ton copper load an' a rocky, rutty
  road,
  An' a evil-minded bunch of mules to go it;
With a leather lash to sting as the sharpest turns I
  swing,
  I haven't any picnic, an' I know it.
'Tis a long an' sudden drop—if I chance to go kerflop
  There wouldn't be much left of me to grumble;
So I finds it very wise just to utilize my eyes,
  For a half a mile is something of a tumble.

I haven't any kick at my chosen daily trick,
  Which you can't exactly value till you've tried it,
But I'd like to have it said that it takes a steady head
  With a pretty fair to middlin' brain inside it.
When the road is hard an' steep an' the yawnin' gulch
  is deep
  An' the space you've got to travel in is narrow,
An' the mules is stubborn brutes, you can bet your
  shirt an' boots
  That you've got to be some stronger than a sparrow.

So I drives 'em day by day down the rough an' crooked
  way,
  An' although it seems I does it helter-skelter,
You can notice, if you will, that I doesn't take a spill,
  An' I gets my load of copper to the smelter.

THE TEAMSTER (continued)

If my language isn't nice—well, you try it once or
  twice
  When the leaders an' the others gets to fussin',
An' you'll find, the same as me, when you try to make
  em "Gee!"
  That a mule was never driven without cussin'.

DRIFTWOOD

CALL me a miner er call me a tramp,
   I've been a little of each,
I've floated into many a camp
   An' drifted upon the beach;
I've drifted from Salt Lake to Jerome,
   The Comstock has knowed me, too.
Wherever I am I calls my home
   An' my trade's whatever I do!

Driftin' along, driftin' along,
Floatin' wherever the tide is strong,
   Goin' no place an' everywhere,
   No one to know an' no one to care,
Gettin' in right er gettin' in wrong—
Driftin', driftin' along.

I'm a Native Son er a Peerless Plug,
   I'm a Notcher, I guess, as well,
An' down in Nevader I have dug
   In heat, hot water an' hell;
High-graded a bit down Goldfield way,
   Gumbooted a bit in Nome.
My habitat is where I stay,
   And wherever I am is home.

Driftin' along, driftin' along,
What do I care if you think it wrong?
   I gets my clothes an' a drink or two,
   An' the rest of my life is nuthin' to you.

DRIFTWOOD (continued)

Floatin' wherever the tide is strong—
Driftin', driftin' along.

Maybe I works a month er so,
   Maybe I works a shift,
An' when I'm ready an' primed to go
   I quits my workin' to drift.
Sometimes I drifts to the county jail,
   An' ceases, sudden, to roam,
Fer I has no cash an' I gets no bail—
   So—wherever I am is home!

Driftin' along, driftin' along,
That's the melody of my song;
   When I dies I reckon I'll drift
   To a hot-box hole an' an endless shift.
But still I'll go where the tide is strong—
Driftin', driftin' along.

THE HARD ROCK MAN

W ELL," I says, "I'm done with minin'
 An' I'll git a job on top,
Where the sun is always shinin',
 An' there ain't no rock to drop.
Nix on that old hard-rock toilin',
 · I will quit an' git a wife,
An' we'll keep the kettle boilin',
 An' I'll settle down fer life."

 Says a friend of mine to me,
 "Honest, bo, you oughta see
This here tunnel we are drivin'—it's a stinger,
  hully gee!
 Yas, I know you've chucked the trade,
 But you needn't be afraid
Fer to come an' look us over with the progress
  we have made."

I was fool enough to listen
 An' they led me to the spot,
Where the air-exhaust was hissin'
 In the headin' wet an' hot,
An' the drills was barkin', barkin',
 An' the mud would spatter high,
An' I found that I was harkin'
 With a tear-drop in me eye.

 An' I wanted to be back
 Where the mule-car rolls the track,

THE HARD ROCK MAN (continued)

> Where you're fightin' rock an' water an' the
>   roof is like to crack;
>   They kin sing of "Mandelay,"
>   An' the "Wanderlust"—but say,
> I kin feel the hard rock fever just a-wastin' me
>   away.

> *Now*, I ain't a blame bit happy
>   In my quiet little job,
> I want drills a-barkin' snappy
>   To the air-compressor's throb;
> An' I want to handle powder
>   An' from job to job to roam,
> Fer the hard rock's callin' louder
>   Than the longin' fer a home.

> Here's a tunnel started new,
> Out near Frisco there are two.
> Oh, a hard rock man can allus find a little
>   work to do;
>   An' I reckon I'm the lad
>   That has got the fever bad,
> An' it oughta make me sorry—but it only
>   makes me glad!

THE PUMPMAN
(As the Miner Sees Him)

NOTHIN' to do but to set around,
   Loafin' a shift away,
The easiest graft that's underground
   An' drawin' the biggest pay.
No sweatin' fer him in a stuffy stope,
   No packin' of drills an' such,
No liftin' of caps on a rotten rope—
   He doesn't amount to much!
There ain't no loose roof waitin' fer him,
   To fall on his bloomin' head;
The gas ain't makin' *his* candle dim,
   Ner makin' *his* eyes all red.
The pumps they chug an' chug an' thump,
   An' he tinkers 'em up a bit,
An' he calls the miner a fat-head chump—
   An' I reckon the miner is *it*.

(As He Sees Himself)

If these brass beauties uv mine shud bust
   I'm thinkin' the gang wud see
How much they've had to put their trust
   In steam, an' the pumps, an' me!
They sees me settin' around so still,
   An' the big pumps hammerin' gay,
But it wudn't take long fer the mine to fill
   If the pumpman went away!

THE PUMPMAN (continued)

It ain't no cinch, but if it was,
    I reckon I've earned it fair,
An' I ain't shovelin' now because
    I'm thinkin' I done my share.
An' now I'm close to the watery sump,
    As I have a right to be,
Tendin' close to the big brass pump,
    The boss of the pump—that's *me!*

SONGS OF THE LONG TRAIL

THE PROPER SETTING

WE sat one night in a dingy bar, that was close to
    the harbor side,
Where we heard the creak of the hawsers thick as the
    ships were swung by the tide,
And the smell of the docks was all about—and the feel
    of the salty air,
We sat in a bar by the harbor edge—the gateway to
    Everywhere.
There was Hogan and Schmitz and Thorpe and Stone,
    Adventurers all were they,
Who had played the game as it should be played—and
    jumped at the chance to play.
They had followed my Lady Adventure's trail wher-
    ever she chose to go,
From the jungle damp and the desert glare to the chill
    of the northern snow,
They had battled and bragged and drunk and loved as
    true tramps royal can,
And they sat in the bar and swapped their yarns—
    the yarns of the rovers' clan;
And banged their fists on the table top, and talked to
    me, man to man.
So I said to myself, "Here is royal sport—to listen to
    men like these,
Who have faced their fate in a hundred lands and
    tempted the Seven Seas;
I will feast them full in my quiet club with a friend
    or two as well,

THE PROPER SETTING (continued)

And we will lounge at the groaning board and hark to
    the tales they tell.
Yes, over the drinks and the cigarettes, while the
    smoke is hanging blue,
We'll hear the chant of the wandertrail, of the men
    who dare and do!"

I gathered my band of roving men and sat them down
    at the feast.
They had come in the stiffest garb they owned with
    trousers neatly creased,
They were nervous and rattled and ill at ease, and
    scarcely a word they spoke,
They wrapped themselves in silence deep and a regu-
    lar pall of smoke.
We knew they were men of dauntless hearts who had
    wandered and ventured far,
But they shut up tight in the sumptuous club and they
    longed for the dingy bar,
They had no fear of the tiger shark, no fright at a
    bullet's screech,
But they were the true Adventurers who could not
    make a speech.

So if you long for the Rovers' tales, drop down where
    the Rovers meet
In a dingy bar near a rotting pier on a shabby harbor
    street.
They'll tell you yarns that will thrill you through with
    the glow of an old delight,
But they won't perform in evening dress at a table
    that's snowy white,

THE PROPER SETTING (continued)

For the saga of true Adventure—and this is the truth
　　you hear,
Is sung the best in a dingy bar with a pipe and a glass
　　of beer.

THE SONG OF THE RAIL

LIFE here in town is too bloomin' monotonous,
    Stickin' around at a regular job,
All the time somebody bossin' or spottin' us,
    Aw, we don't fit in a laborin' mob;
Things here is much too precise and pernickety,
      Bo, I would just as soon be in a jail;
Us for the road an' the wheels that go "clickety,
    Clickety click" on the glimmerin' rail!

Us for the road an' the old hobo way again,
    Loafin' along in the wind an' the sun,
Sleepin' at night in the soft of the hay again,
    Nary a worry of work to be done;
Say, ain't you ready to beat it, by crickety,
    Jump on a freight an' be off on the trail,
Hearin' the music of wheels goin' "clickety,
    Clickety click" on the glimmerin' rail?

Judges'll call us a shame to society,
    Brakeman'll bounce us off onto the ground,
Trampin's no cinch—but it's full of variety,
    Here, we're just ploddin' around an' around!
Honest, I'm gettin' all feeble an' rickety.
      Say, bo, we'll wither up sure if e stick;
Let's hop a rattler with wheels that go "clickety,
    Clickety, clickety, clickety click!"

THE WANDER TRAIL

UP across the mountains, downward through the
vale,
Out upon the foaming seas runs the wander trail;
Pack your bundle, comrade, and take your staff in
hand;
We're off to seek contentment, which dwells in No
Man's Land.
The skies are blue above us, the roaming wind is
sweet,
The roads are warm and springy beneath our faring
feet;
Oh, leave the home-kept people to work and play and
breed—
We must be off, fulfilling the rovers' easy creed!

For lands we've never traveled, for seas we've never
crossed,
Our hearts are all a-hunger, we never count the cost;
The sun in all his glory of rising at the dawn
But calls to us to follow, where he is leading on,
And when, in sheen and splendor, he sinks beneath the
sea,
He seems to send a message, "Come, comrades, follow
me!"
The end of all our journey, who knows what it may
bring?
But friend, the wander fever has wakened with the
spring!

CHANT ROYAL OF THE TRAMP ROYAL

STRANGER, I thank you, now I've cleaned my
    plate,
  It's fine of you to feed a wanderin' guy
That happens to be knockin' at yer gate
  Weary an' faint, without a cent to buy.
That grub has braced me up. I'm gettin' gray,
An' I can't fast like when I was a gay
An' joyous youngster crammed with energy
  Who swaggered down the road in careless glee
In days that's gone an' passed beyond recall
  When I set out an' cried back recklessly,
"The world is wide an' I ain't seen it all!"

I worked at many jobs, an' some was straight
  An' some was crooked as a crooked lie,
An' yet no place could hold me, soon or late
  I'd shake its dust; fer somethin' in the sky
  Er in the winds kept callin' to me. Say,
  When once you hear those voices thataway
There ain't no promise an' there ain't no fee
Kin hold you quiet, you are out of key
  With home-kept folk, your job begins to pall,
An' so I'd quit, with this my only plea,
  "The world is wide an' I ain't seen it all!"

At first my road ran only state to state,
  City to city when the pay was high;
I'd beat my way by passenger er freight,
  There wasn't much that missed my eager eye.

CHANT ROYAL OF THE TRAMP ROYAL (continued)

But when I see a vessel where she lay
Along the dock in San Francisco bay
I shipped aboard her, longin' fer to flee
To strange far lands of myth an' mystery,
An' though the life would cause yer flesh to crawl
I learned a lot—but still my cry must be,
"The world is wide an' I ain't seen it all!"

To keep on goin' was my restless fate;
I couldn't quit an' didn't care to try,
Fer there was things to view both small an' great,
Lands where you freeze an' countries where you fry,
Deserts like brass an' islands drenched in spray,
Queer hidden places where the pilgrims stray,
An' men an' women, Malay an' Chinee,
Christian an' heathen, high an' low degree,
Fightin' an' lovin' on this "earthly ball";
What wonder I obeyed my youth's decree,
"The world is wide an' I ain't seen it all!"

Yes, there was women wanted me to wait,
But I—I heard the voice that drowned their cry,
It's not fer me to settle down an' mate,
The wander fever's got me till I die.
Soft hands might clutch me but I couldn't stay,
There was the road to go, the game to play;
An' though the children clamber on my knee
To hear my tales, there's none belongs to me,
None that will lift me kindly when I fall,
All that I have is life—an' liberty,
The world is wide an' I ain't seen it all!

ENVOY

Stranger, my thanks an' best regards to ye
Fer kindness and fer welcome warm an' free,
 But—there's the road, I can't shake off its thrall,
An' there's so far to go—so much to see;
 The world is wide an' I ain't seen it all!

THE PIONEERS

THEY'RE the "utterly foolish dreamers,"
   Who dream of a better day;
They're not the plotters and schemers
   Who work for glory and pay,
But with confidence undiminished
   They dream of a world made new,
And after their days are finished
   The wonderful dream comes true!

They're the fighters who fight undaunted
   For the utterly hopeless cause,
Ridiculed, jeered and taunted,
   With never a lull or pause;
But after they've fought and perished,
   And after their work is done,
The cause they have loved and cherished
   Is lifted to fame—and won!

They know the hope and the yearning,
   The sting of the blind world's scorn,
But never the sunshine burning,
   The skies of their visioned morn;
They're the warriors fine and splendid,
   The fond and the faithful few,
Whose battles and work are ended,
   Or ever the dreams come true!

AUTUMN MAGIC

FROST on the trees—on the grass,
  A lilt to the steps that pass;
Tang in the air—a breeze
Waking an old unease;
Haze when the day's begun,
  Dawn that is brisk and chill,
Challenge and zest in the sun,
  Setting the blood athrill!
Fall!—and the ducks are flying
  South on their ancient route,
Hear them calling and crying!
  Hunter—come out! Come out!

Fall—and the forest places
  Harbor the leaping deer,
Think of those wooded spaces,
  Think of the campfire's cheer!
The sound, sweet sleep, the lisp
Of the leaves in the wind, the crisp
  And cleanly smell of the pines;
Then the thrill of the chase—to find
  The track of a buck; the signs
Of his light-foot path, and to read
His ways; and to pit your mind
  Against the sight and the scent
And the wariness and speed
Of the wild free thing you stalk:
  Then the shot—and the proud content

AUTUMN MAGIC (continued)

Of bringing your prize to camp;
And, after the sturdy tramp,
Supper and smoke and—talk.
Ah, that is living indeed!
Why do you wait and doubt?
Hunter—come out! Come out!

Fall—and a sapphire sky,
   And your blood in a flood that races,
And the call of the ducks that fly,
   And the lure of the hunting places!
Fall—and the air's astir
With the tingle of life—the whirr
Of a myriad myriad wings
And the movement of wild wild things!
Fall—and the call to you
To come as you used to do
Back on the good old route,
Hunter—come out! Come out!

OUR LADY OF CHANGE

SOMETIMES she's a merry young hoyden,
  A madcap—fair brimming with fun—
Till sudden she shifts in her fancy and lifts
  The sober gray eyes of a Nun;
Her moods are as wayward as winds are,
  They change like the leaping of flame,
And for all of the grace of her form and her face,
  She's never exactly the same!

Sometimes she's a priestess and sibyl
  With eyes that are brooding and sad,
Or a gypsy girl fair with a rose in her hair,
  Or the laughing young Love of a lad,
Sometimes she's Our Lady of Sorrows
  Who's drunken of life to the lees,
Or a Will-o'-the-wisp just as light as the lisp
  Of the leaves of the whispering trees.

I've found her as true as a mother,
  I've known her as false as a jade,
As proud and serene as a panoplied queen,
  As simple and sweet as a maid—
So here's to My Lady Adventure
  Whose magic I may not defy,
By hill and by hollow her footsteps I follow,
  And so I shall do till I die!

ULYSSES

ULYSSES was a rover, a roamer and a rover
    Who sought for high adventure about the sound-
        ing sea,
Who roistered and philandered and fought the wide
    world over,
    And lived a life tempestuous and free.

Ulysses was a rover, a roamer and a rover,
    While I am but a stay-at-home with never chance
        to flee,
But when I dream of wandering the wide world
    blithely over
    The spirit of Ulysses wakes in me.

Ulysses was a rover, a roamer and a rover,
    And when my hopes are realized and all my dreams
        come true,
I'll roister and philander and fight the wide world over
    The way that old Ulysses used to do.

THE RESTLESS LEGION

WE'RE off to the end of the world again,
    We're off on another trail,
Away from the crowded towns of men
    And the airs that are sick and stale;
There's a job at the end of the world for us,
    So we're done with our labor here,
And it's pack your grip for the outward trip,
    We're off to the New Frontier,
And it's "Well, so long!" to the toiling throng.
    We're off to the New Frontier.

It's off to the land of dreams we are,
    Somewhere on the Seven Seas.
Do we go in Peace, do we go in War?
    Well, that's as the Fates may please.
There may be a King to fight with us
    Or a jungle for us to clear;
Whatever the game it's all the same,
    We're off to the New Frontier;
We're primed all right for work or fight,
    We're off to the New Frontier!

We're off again on a long, long chance
    To the lands beyond the law.
We're off in search of the True Romance
    And the realms that are new and raw;
There is much still waits for the white man's eyes
    And the feet of the pioneer;

THE RESTLESS LEGION (continued)

So we're off once more to distant shore,
   We're off to the New Frontier.
And we shout "So long!" to the toiling throng,
   We're off to the New Frontier!

WOMEN

THERE'S pretty girls in every port
　　That fronts upon the foam,
For I've made love in Labrador,
　　In Cairo and in Rome;
I've kissed the girls of London Town
　　And sweet to kiss were they,
But Burmah girls are just as sweet
　　And Frisco girls as gay!

There's always eyes to sparkle bright
　　And hearts a-beating warm,
There's lips the man who's bold may kiss
　　And waists to fill an arm;
The maids are fair in Argentine
　　And dainty in Japan,
There's girls to love in all the world,
　　If you're a proper man.

And who's the fairest of the fair?
　　Well, hang me if I know!
Sometimes I think she lives in France,
　　Sometimes in Callao;
But take 'em north and take 'em south,
　　And take 'em east and west,
Of all the girls in all the world!
　　The last one is the best!

SONGS OF THE TRUE ROMANCE

BOHEMIA

I'M looking for Bohemia,
  Where hearts are ever kind,
Where all the folk are young and poor
  And no one seems to mind;
I'm looking for Bohemia,
  The glad, the ever gay,
Where faith and hope are verities,
Where undiscovered merit is.
Won't some one tell me where it is
  And point me out the way?

I'm looking for Bohemia,
  Where men are leal and true,
Where one may know the rosemary
  And never taste the rue;
I'm looking for Bohemia,
  Where joy has her abode.
Oh, I have heard how fair it is,
How filled with "do and dare" it is.
Can some one tell me where it is
  And put me on the road?

I'm looking for Bohemia,
  The land of heart's desire,
Where love is made of tenderness
  And not of tears and fire;
I'm looking for Bohemia
  Despite the cynics' doubt

BOHEMIA (continued)

(An idle dream, they swear it is,
The truth I still declare it is).
Won't some one tell me where it is
    And set me on the route?

I'm looking for Bohemia,
    I've sought it far and long:
The place of ever-wreathing smoke,
    Of laughter, love and song.
I'll not believe Bohemia
    Is only dream-stuff frail.
Ah, surely more than air it is,
In some Elysian lair it is,
And I shall learn of where it is
    And follow on the trail!

TO A PHOTOGRAPHER

I HAVE known love and hate and work and fight;
  I have lived largely, I have dreamed and planned,
  And Time, the Sculptor, with a master hand
Has graven on my face for all men's sight
Deep lines of joy and sorrow, growth and blight
  Of labor and of service and command
  —And now you show me this, this waxen, bland
And placid face, unlined, unwrinkled, white.

This is not I—this fatuous thing you show,
  Retouched and smoothed and prettified to please,
Put back the wrinkles and the lines I know;
  I have spent blood and tears achieving these,
Out of the pain, the struggle and the wrack
These are my scars of battle—put them back!

THE REFORMER

DOES it make you mad when you read about
  Some poor, starved devil who flickered out
Because he had never a decent chance
In the tangled meshes of circumstance?
If it makes you burn like the fires of sin,
Brother, you're fit for the ranks—fall in!

Does it make you rage when you come to learn
Of a clean souled woman who could not earn
Enough to live and who fought, but fell
In the bitter struggle and went to hell?
Does it make you seethe with an anger hot?
Brother, we welcome you, share our lot!

Whoever has blood that will flood his face
At the sight of the Beast in the holy place;
Whoever has rage for the tyrant's might,
For the powers that prey in the day and night;
Whoever has hate for the ravening brute,
That strips the tree of its goodly fruit;
Whoever knows wrath at the sight of pain,
Of needless sorrow and heedless gain;
Whoever knows bitterness, shame and gall
At the thought of the trampled ones doomed to fall;
He is a brother-in-blood, we know,
With brain afire and with heart aglow;
By the light in his eyes we sense our kin,
Brother, you battle with us—fall in!

THE SONG OF THE AERONAUT

UP from the emerald turf I rise to the lure of the
  arching blue,
With a song in my heart like the ancient song the
  great Olympians knew.
While I steady myself on wings of white to the rush
  of the roving breeze,
Tempting the wrath of the infinite, the marvelous
  weightless seas;
Below me the world is a blur of green, a flicker of
  brown and red,
And the vault of the sky is mine to try and the limit-
  less vast ahead!
It's sport that only the birds have known who poise
  in the upper day,
But now I challenge their airy throne—these kings of
  the blue highway!

I buffet my route through winds that shout, I dip to
  the billows of air,
And mock me the hawk and the pirate bird that hover
  in wonder there.
Disdainful I sweep above mortals who creep like
  worms on the overturned clod,
And serenely I soar in the empire of space—an inso-
  lent, strong-winged god!
The purr of the motors, the shiver of wires and the lift
  of the quivering planes,
As I clamber the sides of aerial hills and swoop down
  aerial lanes,

THE SONG OF THE AERONAUT (continued)

Stir all my blood to a turbulent flood till all that is
    earthly of me
Is lost in a rapture of speed and of flight—I am free,
    I am free, I am free!

For mine is no road that is meted and bound, but the
    way of the wind and the sky,
Beyond all the dust and the fret and the heat, above
    all the clamor I fly
To the height where the hawk circles wary and lone,
    to the vault where the bald eagles scream,
Where the fetters of earth and the worries of earth are
    dim in the haze of a dream.
Then sudden I drop toward the world I have left and
    the wind whistles keen through the frame,
Or I wheel and I swing in a glorious ring on a trail
    that is never the same.
Oh, danger is mine in this frolic divine as I dare all
    the forces that slay,
But mine is the song of the free and the strong—the
    Lord of the Blue Highway!

THE DESERTER

YOU can put me into irons for my durn fool crime,
  You can make me scrub an' labor for a long, long
    time,
You can set me scrapin' turrets in the hot, hot sun,
You can make me scrape another when that job is
    done;
Yes, I'll pay my penance gladly, for I've got my sense,
An' I'll charge the pain an' trouble to experience.
I went an' I deserted like a plain fool Jack;
I was weary of the navy—Thank the Lord I'm back!

I was sick of young Lieutenants an' of non-coms too,
An' I thought myself a member of a poor slave crew,
I didn't like the duties or the dis-cip-pline,
An' I thought I was mistreated on the salty brine,
So I chucked away an' beat it, I was smooth, you bet,
If I hadn't come here willin' you'd be searchin' yet,
But Gosh, how clean the ship is, nothin' skimped or
    slack,
It was me that quit the navy—an' it's me that's back!

Yes, I had my taste of freedom an' it lasted quick,
I met a lot of hoboes an' they made me sick,
I found a lubber's labor wasn't nothin' grand,
An' I didn't care fur cussin' 'stead of stern command,
My bunks was somethin' awful an' my food was rot,
An' I missed my little hammock an' the mess we got,
I was scared of bein' captured on most every tack,
An'—Lord, but I was filthy, so I just came back!

THE DESERTER (continued)

You can put me into irons, I don't give a damn,
I am back again in service of my Uncle Sam,
An' I've got a navy outfit an' my body's clean,
An' in time I'll win my place back in the big machine,
With its rules an' regulations, with its work an' play,
With its drills an' guns an' spirit, an' its good sure pay,
With its beatin' round the oceans on the broad sea
    track,
—Oh, I'll get it, good an' plenty, but I'm glad I'm
    back!

THE ·MOTHER

SURE, an' I'm waitin' to hear but the step av him,
  Him that's been gone from us year afther year,
He will come back like the picture I've kep' av him
  Smilin' an' gay wid his mirth an' his cheer.
Thrue, they are sayin' it's death that has taken him,
  But I know betther that knew him so well,
An' it's meself will be huggin' an' shakin' him
  Whin he comes back wid fine sthories to tell.

Whin the wind whistles I think it's the trill av him
  —That was the way he would do whin he came,—
Why do you sit there an' talkin' so ill av him,
  Sayin' he's dead? It shud fill ye wid shame;
Yes, I remimber him lyin' here stilly-like,
  But he was foolin' ye, women an' men,
'Twas but a prank av him, foolish an' silly-like,
  Sure, he'll be back to his mother again.

Whin the door rattles I think, " 'Tis the hand av him
  Feelin' around fer the latch in the dark,
Whin he comes in I'll be cross an' demand av him
  Why he stayed out so late havin' a lark."
So, all the time I am harkin' an' listenin',
  Hearin' each step an' each sound in the gloam,
Sure, me old eyes wid the tear drops are glistenin'
  Thinkin' how glad I'll be whin he comes home!

THE GHOST OF PETE McCLUSKEY

THE ghost of Pete McCluskey came aknockin' on
the door.
"Come in; come in," I says to him; "but do not thrack
the floor—
'Tis newly washed this afthernoon"—an' then I shuk
wid fright,
For Peter stud before me an' the door still fastened
tight.

"Resoomin' av our argyment the night before I died,"
Said Pete McCluskey then to me, asittin' by my side,
"I've wandhered round the universe in spiritual guise,
An' since I died I find I am particularly wise;
An' I have thought av argyments that certainly is
strong,
An' so I came to talk to ye an' show ye where ye're
wrong."

I thried to speak, but not a word wud issue from me
lip,
While Pete McCluskey opened up an' let his language
rip.
He may have sailed the universe, but what he didn't
learn
Wud fill a library or two, with stuff besides to burn;
His argyments was futile rot for all he was a ghost.
I hope I'll have more brains than Pete when I am with
the host.

THE GHOST OF PETE McCLUSKEY (continued)

But nary word cud I put in while he went on an' on,
Explainin' foolish argyments till I was pale an' wan;
He shuk his finger, slapped his knee, an' talked an'
    talked some more,
An' though I am a patient man I sure was gettin' sore;
His postulates was very bad, his premises was worse,
An' yet I cudn't shut him up or answer him or curse.

As dawn came on he started off, asayin' as he went:
"Now this is what I surely call a pleasant argyment.
You haven't had a word to say; I take it you agree
With all I've said?—to argue thus is Heaven enough
    for me.
Why shud I tap at Heaven's gate when this is just as
    well?"
"It may be Heaven for you," I says; "but, Pete, for me
    it's hell."

Then Pete he smiles an' disappears; but when he came
    again
I had a dozen Socialists to help me out, an' then
They put poor Peter on the blink; it was a bitter cup.
But even ghostly sophistries cud never shut them up.

It broke his heart, an' though he comes an' knocks
    upon the door
He sits an' never says a word, while I—I have the
    floor.
An' if you happen round at night you probably will see
The ghost of Pete McCluskey always listenin' to me!

THE ADVENTURER

CITY of power and city of might,
　　Of plunder and passion and woe and delight,
The sound of your voice is a trumpeter's blare,
A challenge that's flung on the palpitant air,
A pæan of battle, a taunt, and a call
To join in the conflict and conquer—or fall,
To thrust and to parry, to feint and to lunge;
So—into the tumult I plunge!

I fear you?—the city of opulent dreams—
Because of your vastness that pulses and teems?
Why, here are my hands, they are young, they are
　　　strong
As any two hands in the thick of the throng;
And here are my eyes and my body and brain
Alert for the glory and gold I shall gain.
So—fearless I face you, O huge, roaring brute,
Besotted with splendor and glutted with loot!

What peril of jungle or desert or sea
Has more of a thrill than your dangers to me,
Or greater romance than the conflict that rolls
On your vast battlefield of a myriad souls?

I cry you defiance! Your masters and slaves,
Your wasters and delvers and dreamers and knaves,
I war for your palaces, pleasures and pelf;
I fear you no whit—for I fear not myself;
I face you and fight you, nor whimper for aid,
Since you crawl to the feet of the man unafraid!

SPRING IN THE CITY

OVER the stones of the city street
 Comes a wind of promise, warm and sweet;
Gently it breathes on the city square
A balm and softness blithe and rare,
A message of Springtide everywhere.
There's a hint o' dreams in the shop-girl's eyes
(So soon grown weary and hard and wise!)
And the old blind beggar is seen to smile,
Making his plea for pence the while;
And the money-grubber becomes less grim
When the glad wind whispers a word to him;
While the slums respond to the tender thrill
As the zephyr sighs at the window-sill.
And the babies coo, and the mothers croon,
And even the street piano's tune
Seems sweet and gay as the pipes o' Pan
In the golden days when the world began!
It needs no green of the turf or trees,
No chirp of robins or hum of bees,
To prove the goddess is on her way;
For over the city, dull and gray,
This wind comes frolicking, fair and free,
A joyous herald of Arcady.
And drudge and wanton and rich and poor
Are summoned alike by the laughing lure,
And we know by the glow in the eyes of men
That Spring's come back to the town again!

THE TELEPHONE DIRECTORY

WHAT is there seeming duller than this book,
   This stolid volume of prosaic print?
And yet it is a glass through which we look
   On wonderland and marvels without stint.
It is a key which will unlock the gate
   Of distance and of time and circumstance,
A wand that makes the wires articulate
   With hum of trade and whisper of romance!

Somehow there is enchantment in each page—
   The whirr of wheels, the murmurs of the mart,
The myriad mighty voices of the age,
   The throbbing of the great world's restless heart,—
Such are the sounds this volume seems to store
   For him who feels the magic of its thrall,
Who views the vistas it unrolls before
   His eyes that scarce can comprehend them all!

Here is the guide to all the vast extent
   The wires have bound together, this will show
The way to help when need is imminent,
   When terror threatens or when life burns low;
This brings the lover to his heart's desire,
   That he may speak to her o'er hill and lea,
This is the secret of the singing wire,
   To all the "world without" this is the key!

THE PHONOGRAPH

I AM the voice of sadness, I am the voice of mirth;
   I carry the magic message to the uttermost ends
      of earth;
And though the critics mock me with many a bitter
      sneer,
Out in the lonely places my song is good to hear,
And what do I care for critics cooped up in a four-
      walled pen?
Out in the desert spaces I comfort the souls of men;
To pioneers on the border the message of Home I
      bring,
By wizardry of a record, a vibrant steel and a spring!

   I stir the heart with old songs
      And light the eyes with new,
   I chant the more-than-gold songs
      Which thrill you through and through;
   The gentle and the bold songs,
      I sing them all to you!

Into the tenement dingy I carry the songs of May,
I bring a flush of color to faces all pinched and gray,
And out in the lonely farmhouse I warble my gayest
      air,
Bringing the voice of the city for the country dwellers
      to share;

THE PHONOGRAPH (continued)

When men are weary of toiling and their hearts are
heavy as lead
I rattle a song in ragtime till the dreariest blues are
fled.
You may say my voice is raucous and the music I
make is "canned,"
But you'll hear me singing my carols in every clime
and land.

I sing the blithe and brave songs,
The songs of East and West,
The mountain and the wave songs,
The love-songs tenderest,
The laughing and the grave songs,
Whatever suits you best.

Now hark to my proclamation, O you of the critic
court!
I have taught more people music than all of your carp-
ing sort.
I have made the work of the Masters, their glorious,
mighty spell,
Not only the rich men's pleasure, but the poor man's
joy as well,
While you, in your cynic wisdom, your poisoned shafts
have hurled,
I have been spreading gladness and beauty over the
world.
In palace and hut and cabin, from pole to the tropic
line,
Wherever your feet may wander, the Voice you will
hear is MINE!

THE PHONOGRAPH (continued)

> With classic and with light songs,
>   With songs of pain and glee,
> With morning, noon or night songs,
>   With songs of land or sea,
> But ever with the right songs,
>   I bring you Arcady!

THE LIVING EPITAPH

WHEN I pass out and my time is spent,
  I hope for no lofty monument,
No splendid procession marching slow,
Along the last long road I go;
No pomp and glory I care for then,
When I depart from the world of men.

But I'd like to think when my race is through
That there will be in the world a few
Who'll say, "Well, there is a good man gone,
I'm sorry to see him passing on,
For he was a sort that's fair and square,
The kind of fellow it's hard to spare.

"He hadn't money, he hadn't fame,
But he kept the rules and he played the game,
His eyes were true and his laugh was clear,
He held his truth and his honor dear.
And now that his work is at an end,
I know how much I shall miss my friend."

If my life shall earn such words as those
I shall smile in peace as my eyelids close,
I shall rest in quiet and lie content,
With the words of a friend for my monument.

CPSIA information can be obtained
at www.ICGtesting.com
Printed in the USA
BVHW06s1516230418
514169BV00032B/1797/P